MAKARRA

MAKARRA

BARRINA SOUTH

RECENT
WORK
PRESS

Makarra
Recent Work Press
Canberra, Australia

Copyright © Barrina South, 2024

ISBN: 9781763670105 (paperback)

A catalogue record for this
book is available from the
National Library of Australia

Cover image: 'Sunrise Through a Rain-Splattered Window' by Ron Cogswell. Reproduced under Creative Commons Licence 2.0
Cover design: Recent Work Press
Internal illustrations: © John South, 2024
Set by Recent Work Press
recentworkpress.com

Produced on Ngunnawal and Ngambri Country.
Indigenous sovereignty was never ceded.

*I dedicate this collection to my Nan,
Florence Edith Payne who was born
on the Brewarrina Mission in 1910. A
beautiful woman who had a gentle soul
and generous heart.*

Contents

When I was 4 years of age in Nyngan, things were falling from the sky. Wet drops, hitting me. I was frightened and cried; it was the first time I had ever seen rain.

Jean South, 2024

Two Stroke

I read in a poem the words *Victor took the jug cord to the boys for years*
one of those poems, one of those lines, that fizzes on the page
words irradiate
dark memories you keep deep inside
hurt that is sharp, to the bone, straight to the heart
on young tender limbs
wooden spoon, wire coat hanger or belt
a fibro garage, one hot afternoon, smell of two stroke
wearing party masks, we spill paint
father appears, firstly slapping the mask off his son's face
my friend anticipated what was to come next
laid in
not like any discipline I knew
held my breath
gut-wrenching howls
his mum watching, smiled
suggesting it was time for me to go home
scared me the most
I ran
on the way a kid yelled out 'Go, Batman Go!'

A Few of My Favourite Things

Dip my arms into hot wax
    smash my shin with a hammer
    tie my long hair to the rafter, drop down and swing

      scrape off the rust with my teeth
      hold a lit match on one eye and an ice cube on the other

  eat a tablespoon of flour
  drink a cup of vinegar

      lick a handful of salt with a cut tongue and ulcered mouth

    insert a long sharp needle into my ear
    hit the other hard with a paddle
    open cheeks with a razor and insert hot coals

      kick the small toe against the bed leg
      slowly peel back my fingernails
      wrap thighs in barb wire and run

These are a few of my favourite things

Black Dark Spaces

Crawl underneath
tip of the nose against the base board
outstretched, quiet
watch feet move in and out of the room
calling my name, I stay still
in this black dark space

    hall cupboard, odds and ends
    switch board, broken chair, empty picture frames
    into the corner at the back
    where the light doesn't reach, I go

    standing among forgotten items
    calling my name, I stay still
    in this black dark space

    small wooden door, on the side of the house
    rarely unlocked
    twist the bolt
    hunched over, then on hands and knees
    fine dirt, house floor beams
    that gradually slope
    I can't push any further
    reach out to touch the foundations
    calling my name, I stay still
    in this black dark space

    when the lights go out
    house in darkness

others fetch torches
while I slide under the dining table, behind the linen tablecloth
sitting on floral carpet
run my fingers on the underside of the table, tracing legs and feet
calling my name, I stay still
in this black dark space

Pretty Knick Knack

You promised to let me go
    suspended in a glass case
    pinned beside collected Christmas beetles and discarded cigarette butts
    a pretty Knick knack

    you would bite me to mark me
    dip your fingers inside
    confirm that I was sick
    place cups upside down
    tell me my future

    you hid me
    measured me from my toes to my head
    marked it on the bathroom wall
    I saw it everyday
    measurement ready at anytime

    you unpicked my hems
    darned all my socks together
    burnt my pressed flowers
    untied the wind chimes
        a pretty knick knack

Things Got Ugly Quickly

Blood bruised thumb nail slices the prawn
extracting the digestive tube
resting against the white marble bench
filleting the fish, in the sun, opalised tiles
dark, purple entrails slip out, lemon juice spills
she leans over, glides her tongue hard against the grain of the fish scales
they stick like barbs
droplets of blood spots the marble
clouded eyes we stare, after the mirror falls
shards find her feet, like an ice skater, glides across the kitchen floor
we finish the claret, blotting our lips with thistle leaves
and watch as things got really, really, ugly quickly

Writers' meeting

She reads the poem every month, every meeting
hoping to get the words out without crying, without stopping
so that one day she can read it in public

today as she spits out the words, the literary purge about her hate for
her mother, produces two lines of blood from her nose
bright red lines slowly make their way to her philtrum where it pools
before flowing around the lips

she continues with her words
the overflow seeps into her mouth
with the taste of copper, realises she is bleeding, the large droplets of
blood now on her notebook, confirm it

as she swallows, the taste has brought to the surface the memories told
to us in her poem about *a young girl biting the inside of the walls of the
mouth. Causing pain, to forget*

she takes the white, ironed, cotton handkerchief from the elderly
writer across from her,
pressing it against her face, it symbolises the second stanza *a lifetime of
being muzzled*
from the writers' circle, a chorus of 'head forward', 'head back',
inadequate advice from those who were there to take care of her
the look of shock on the face of the others, symbolic of lines *people
knew, no one said anything, no one helped*

next month she will ask to read the poem again
hoping to get the words out without crying, without stopping

Flare Up

Knowing it will hurt
I still pump the soap dispenser

palms wince

the switch is flicked
beneath the skin
feeling of hot coiled elements blistering
a flare up
now red, raw and sore

then,   **the urge**
take a deep breath
pacify with a fatty balm
inner voice warns, 'Don't do it'.

I run one finger across, softly

countdown begins, then
launch into a feverish solitude, unhealthy craving to be filled with
   excess scratching

in a moment of lucidity, recite my mantra

only until the urge goes
only until the skin breaks
only until I bleed

but the circle has begun

Curtain

TV's neon eye blinks
sending light around the room
a sour smell of a dog's underbelly
whisper of cool air across my feet
rest of my body, hot
tongue coated in gin
dog stirs, so does he, lying beside me
sheer curtain rises
draws back on the breeze
it is that time of night
across the street, top apartment light flicks on
I make my way to the window
sheet around my shoulders drops
stay just long enough
until the light flicks off
before the dog
moves
and he wakes

Beneath a Green Glass Surface

His breath pushing, gliding through slumber
our routine well practiced

What is it to lie beside another?
just beneath a green glass surface
guard down, at our most vulnerable

> awake, my star
> like a clock's hour hand slowly ticking anticlockwise
> taking comfort knowing the stars are always there
>
> fan dances in the corner
> I should bring in another but who am I to assume it needs a partner
>
> her wish to forever dance, alone
> rusted red Kangaroo paws in bloom
> I place one in the back of the fan's guard
> with flower, she continues to dance
> back and forth

Long Weekend

Silver Banksia pods with drowsy eyes, dreaming on coastal winds
desire to taste the salt and sweat on your shoulders across my tongue
thighs await the weight of your hand, toes dig into wet sand

all night the lightning shook as we caught our breath
the sky drenches the thirsty earth
desire to taste and smell the salt on your shoulders across my tongue

floating on foaming surface, under smudged ash coloured storm clouds
rhythm of the waves cradling me
the sky drenches the thirsty earth

guided by your hand, step down on to the soft sand
walking ancient pathways to the sea
rhythm of the waves cradling me

with a feather you scoop the stars from the night sky and place them in
    my hair
with a whole heart, walk beside you now and forever
walking ancient pathways to the sea

mauve and golden sky, I listen to the birth of a new day
silver Banksia pods with drowsy eyes, dreaming on coastal winds
while we entwine in the dawn light, water's glare
thighs await the weight of your hand, toes dig into wet sand

Afternoon light

Light comes in on an angle through the window
picking up forgotten surfaces
brushstrokes left on freshly painted windowsills
deep scratch across wooden floorboards
light alters the everyday into something special
glint off a glass rim leaves a halo on the bench
catch my breath at the fragility of a fallen petal
savour mottled shadows dancing on the cornices
you lean back
branch lightly scrapes the lead glass pane
afternoon golden light on your lips

Unfinished

Cool damp air
finds bare thighs
warm palms slide

my hands dig deep
into sandstone grit
last of the light
lilac shadows
contours of
armpits and pelvic bone

I take Country home to bed
in my hair and on the soles of my feet

Kiira-Kiira

She brings me the bones
I sit on the ground
I fidget

    We sit
    not time

She looks up
wedge tails soar, circle, rise
I count the hours past and hours left

    not time
our hands rest across knees

    inhale, exhale
stale breath leaves me

rain marks skin
old songs are sung
moon rises
vibrating with beat

ngiyi wiimpatya
kiira-kiira
ngiyi wiimpatya
kiira-kiira
the bones are in my hands

Cockatoos

My eyes caress his limbs
diaphanous droplets
glisten like a crown on the canopy

I press against the cool bark

from the valley floor

    whee-la   *whee-la*

                                                          whee-la

a mournful cry that has
circled all day
bringing makarra

some land heavy
loosen the jewels
that shower down
onto the nape of my neck

others crack pinecones

a glimpse of a yellow blush cheek
I eavesdrop on clicks and chatter
envious of their gentle allopreening

as they leave
believing I can touch their sombre underbellies
reach out

                                              I am home

Ghost Gum

Upon the once young creamy, pink-tinged skin
pooled blood appears
caused by previous contusions
leaving her discoloured

      recent lesions continue haemorrhaging
      old sores still weeping
      the disfigured and swollen skin
      now tight
      shiny, ready to split

   her veins draw the healing sap to the surface
   to medicate all wounds
   seasonally white, powdery, bark scales
   shed
   stolen by the hot wind
      saucer like seeds fall out of wide-open woody mouths
      of those who sing, as they regurgitate
      the beginning of another

in the cool of the night
respite

      she reaches up and gently sways
      dancing in time with the stars
      as they sweep across the desert night sky

Kurrajong

Branches heavy with promises left by lovers who press against
　　　her canopy whispers back
　　　　　　all are lost to the night
quiet
cold
still
leaves sparkle under streetlights
　　　she sings a lullaby to sooth us all to sleep

hot summer days she takes up the whole sky
watches over us
school students pass under while dignitaries pass by
　　　she is all knowing, offers so much
　　　　　　longing to be touched to make nets and string
contented to ring pink bells for spring
rain glosses her leaves, turning them a deep green
wooden seed pods ahull down deep gutters
she smiles as we duck and weave

other times sorrowful because most do not see
our beauty in our street

Baaka

Bulging banks, sodden with water
nature's refuse washes away downstream
dry branches bounce, to the rhythm of the current
ripples form,
turn
and disappear
tree trunks, freshly painted with the river flow
turn to marble

scars made by the Old people, reminders of past floods
farm fences invade the river and straight up the other side
they fence the rivers too

crumpled water tanks lie on their sides
kerosene tins
bed frames
broken glass remains, in memorial to those who once lived by the Baaka

listen carefully

you can imagine the women from the Mission
talking
as they care for their children playing in the river
a place of respite from the government gaze
and control

Godoomba

I was here
marked only by the words on the page
abstention from the outside world
affording space for deep listening

Godoomba, Godoomba
Godoomba, Godoomba

words roll lightly across my tongue
drinking it in like sweet water
from the swollen banksia flowers after the rain

words wake a conversation, a susurration
that comes up from deep within the valley floor
they remember, I have been here before
a long time ago

body is sore, assailed by doubts
caused by unsympathetic orators of past critics
time spent lamenting
for unfinished poems

that sit
just outside my window
hanging in the morning mist
just out of reach
or stolen at dusk
carried on the antiphonal call of the currawongs

Shifting

I wait
to be

                                        Welcomed

    standing in front
    silently, trace Country
    linger
    in the margins
    with trained eye
    measure, assess, count

    no signs

    wait

    disorientated
    nature's magnetic forces askew
    to understand

                                        connect

    I step through the gilded frame
    canvas stretches
    feet slip across oil

    on the other side
    dark, temperature drops
    a state of estivation

                                        awake

cool undercurrent off the high winds
brings the smell of rain
watch the storm move across the sky
high enough to grasp the stars

from the valley floor
I hear a cry that has
circled all day

lone dingo howl
pulls down the last of the

light

a shiver runs down my spine
a spool losing its ribbon

sit
hands rested on knees
fingers gently dip into

Country

in my mind's eye
trace well-worn paths

inhale

the smoke of the gum leaves

feed on the dark syrup of yams
listen to women sing

as the storm is about to swallow us

whole

and I am lost to the mountains
imprint granite tors
with an open palm

push myself back through the gilded frame

standing in front
orientated
at ease
magnetic forces

aligned

Untitled

I remember the day the sky died
arms hung heavy from my shoulders
feet were slow to move
head too heavy to lift
I would reach the edge, it was going to take time
focussed on the horizon
aim to keep moving
temptation to lie down
conjuring up courage, forced myself to fall
face down, grit coats my lips
dust filling my nostrils
waiting, hoping someone might discover me before it got dark

Writers' Space

Cold February air grabs
the back of my neck

    we snuff the fire coals
    fold the bedding

    grateful for the fruit trees
    who nourished us
    salute the ghost gums
    who stood guard
    protecting us at our most vulnerable

        six bundles of manuscripts
        stacked by the front door

we step out into the dark

    leaving the halcyon nest
    of woven wisteria and clematis

Windows

ABC radio, crystal in the window
shallow breathing, waiting
sitting in a plastic covered chair

red taillights against a jet-black night
air brakes of trucks descending the mountain
growl that always turns my stomach
legs stretching across cold sheets, in an over tucked bed

a dog yelps in pain

shelves of books, faded spines and fingered pages
erotic tales, tender love
believing they have invented lust and longing
each story, like biting into a warm plum
just fallen, laying in the morning sun

Patricia arrives; I learn that staring through windows at strangers is fine
if done with longing and at a distance
and you should never trust the stranger who invites you in

looking in, looking out
peering, scrutinising phrases and words
fold in the ones that resonate to fluff up stale poems, left to go rancid on
    the screen

silence, busy minds and words not spoken
thoughts untested by tongue, untested on ears and not given time to cure
unzip my skull and tip out the letters

let them fall like scrabble tiles, clinking on a glass table and off the edge
into the unknown

First Day Back

Tamped by the pings of emails, all urgent
dull buzz of incoming texts and missed calls
just like that, misophonia is back
I become raw, red, sore
trapped looking at a square screen
tethered to a square desk

                                                        behind a square window
rain taps against the leaves
turning the Lomandra into ribbons of polished greenstone
new soft leaves of the Callistemons turn silver
delicate droplets glisten

I stand up, climb out
my scaffold, Callistemon
kick off my sandals
wet leaves sticky

laying down in the foliage
rain spots my skin
first, it's cold, but the longer I stay
I settle

drenched, it is hard to tell
where the body ends, and the earth begins
the soaked soil, a fatty balm
I climb back through the window
and into sleep

Cloth

A piece of cloth has caught my eye
hooked on the barb wire
trying to be free, flapping in Morse, help me
it gives up its fight
when the wind leaves it alone
faded, a captive for some time
loose thread flies on its own a sign of hope for the others

Walking

Nature is waiting for me
gust greets me with open arms
a wall of heat
grasses heavy with seed bounce
a plane leaves a chalk line across a cloudless sky
one of those days

> dry leaves run on the wind
> a siren
> memories of this time three years ago
> sends a shudder
> like a skink whose sun bath is disturbed

> but bees continue to draw on nectar
> while wrens dance

The Gift

Navy and white sun beds
foxtail palm fronds sway
in time with the prattle
repetitive well-rehearsed lines of banal life events over
platters of tropical fruit, turning in the hot sun
forgotten soft cheeses
furtive glance between couples, furling damp towels, furrowed brows as
    wives laugh too loud

temptation to slip into a state of torpor in the ice at the bottom of the
    frozen cocktail
passerine birds quietly watch, as I loosen the guy rope of the cabana
unmoored, I drift taking my son's hand towards the sound of the waves
buoyant on our backs, our feet hang, dragging lightly across the sea floor
water changes from turquoise to dark blue

the island calls us

sea turtles paddled-shaped arms, guide us straight to the calm of the bay
on their way to the feeding grounds off the strait
water becomes warmer and muddy, they leave us
my son and I slip on the drift of a mother whale suckling her calf
catching up, we count the barnacles and scars
mothers stare knowingly into each other's eyes
lung full of air, a spray, dissipates, they dive deep for true north

we find ourselves in shallow water
among the spotted stingrays and coloured fish
the trough has brought us safely here

our palms slap the water
then lightly graze over heavily harvested oyster shelled rocks
on the beach, toes trace the fine lines, left by marooned seaweed and crabs
   retreating
we stand side by side, watch the last of a wave's life
my son hands me a gift of a seashell

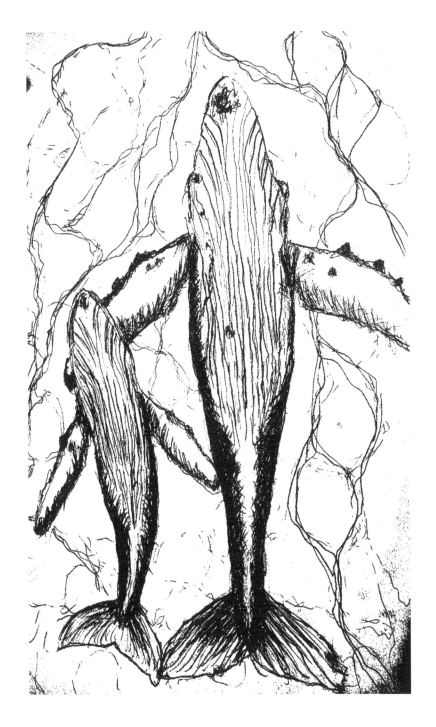

Graphite

Knees on leaf litter
beside the base
of Giants
from this position
the rain seeps through
there, for not animal or plant
but messengers that heal and speak to all
standing proud in purple, orange and yellow
black, blue and green
strike, curl, smudge and hatch
days and days spent on Country
captured in 2B and 4B graphite
by the wild river, I wept

Grief is Love

A lone cockatoo cries out
keening
that pulls down the last of the light

    my days
    are nights
    my nights
    are   awake

    I stare at my reflection
    ghostly self-portrait by the lamp light
    pinturas negras

    count my breath
    like I counted the rise and fall of your hospital sheet
    grief is love

    the house
    no longer a home
    you are not here
    to guide my feet
    lift my robe

    11.33pm.
    No missed messages

a bogong moth
attracted by a false moon
assiduous in his feverish distraction

scrawled hallowed words on cards
stoic on the mantle
constant reminder

5.33am.
No missed messages

a lone cockatoo cries out
keening

I Own a Stone

I own a stone
it sits in the pit of my soul
made from all the grief grit

I've watched it grow
in stagnate silt
I try to lift it
gravity keeps it in place

She says I have an obstacle
I remind her about the stone
this time she writes it down

a ballast
sometimes it sits low
cradled in my pelvis
stone against bone
pressure on tendons

I own a stone
a stone of grief grit
a stone that will continue to grow
when I finally lay down
it will click into place

when I go the stone will remain
catch your eye and you will pick it up
add it to the collection of stones
that sit on the windowsill

Weereewa

Respectfully yuma weereewa
filled from the rain
lost under the sun

> restricted flow
> shallow
> but with a deep history

evidence suspended in the silt
pollen and ash
worked stone

> eagles circle, watching
> lake's large mouth, calls
> its tongue licks at the foreshore

He sits, looking up from below
careful, he waits
for those who take what is not for the taking

> sorrow trees recline in the water-soaked reeds
> weathered arms outstretched beckoning us to come sit
> heal a scarred soul or

> damaged heart

I sit cradled by the woody arms
they whisper the message of peace, forgiveness, and love

Suit of Lucency

Darkening the sun everyday
I see you
in a crack of Mount Zion wall

smothered in a man's suit of lucency
you carve
with screwdrivers and cold chisels
of Parrot Fish, bleeding

we cycle, in
all is calm and comfort

a mesmerised commissariat
exercising their cowed, shaven souls
Some things change, some stay the same

Oak Trees and Gum Trees

Modest conversations with
      interruptions
      static
      broken sentences
and silence

I ask her to read to me
100 poems
by 100 poets
she does
while tying crystals to my ankles

      I sink

like a ghostly shipwreck
settled on the ocean floor

slowly running out of breath
she lies with me
amongst the shells, Bream jaw bones and coral

similar but
different
oak trees and ghost gums
northeast and southeast

The Lake

Laying down tools
ants assemble
set sail vacated cicada shells onto the lake
signal a night of hedonism

                                        keeps her laughing

magpies hunt for moths
put them to sleep in their nests
for the Portuguese millipedes to
bottle their powdery scales
for blowing into the clouds
turn them grey

                                        keeps her full

sorrow trees collect on their splintered limbs
white fur of the soft footed roos
felted, when pulled across echidna trains
now a blanket
carried on the eagle's talons
folded in

                                        keeps her warm

blue wrens recline in webs
spiders comb them
collecting hues
to be scattered
under a full moon

                                        keeping her blue

Paper boats

At dusk
we launch paper boats
with the free-flowing words
inscribed in charcoal
last of the daylight
allows us to watch
them set sail into the night
we wait for the water to swallow them
solace knowing our words will dissolve
lay in the silt
fossilised for future voices to read and ponder

Picture Card

He kissed a photo of his mum
I swept red sand, ash
of home
we could not hold back

Sitting
Playing cards
safe
there was only one mouthful left

Despite the crimson on their faces
I saw
starved parrots
sing

Purple Stockings

The six of us came together, to change the world
stood on tables, and bared our purple stockings
made mischief of all kinds to
disrupt, question and educate, calling *Viva E vulva ing Revolution!*
the masses shouted "you have nothing to say, go home and look after
your children".
we fought back, carved our message into walls, penned manifesto,
created canvases, and stated it in poems

    then one day   the six of us laid down
    to gather energy to keep up the fight
    no one looked for us or questioned the silence
    we laid in the gum leaves, days came and went
    mycena interupta grew over our eyes and mycena pura grew out
        our ears
    our hair covered in gum flowers stamens heavy in nectar and scent,
        golden yellow and crimson red, pansies bloomed and went
    mycelium and hyphae grew across our chests, sending messages
        through bioelectrical signs to wake

    'End capitalism!' rang through the air, we awoke to a new world
    emphasis on networks, collegiality, and collaboration rather than
        hierarchy
    share/share economy and more public spaces
    intergenerational equity and nature now had rights
    adoption of radical municipality and an UBI
    no gender binaries, only spectrum

even though our stockings had faded, they shouted our names
held a parade, recited our mantras from moss covered walls
mouldy manifesto, faded art and forgotten poems
and thanked us for fighting for a new future, one that was better
   for us all
no matter how big or how small

We

after Gwendolyn Brooks

When no one wants us anymore, We
seek out our Own, those who really understand, what is real
abandoned children, bruised, molested, stinkin' and starved, don't let on,
   be cool
otherwise, you stand out, become prey, We
stick by each other, all that's left
learn quick, the rules of street school
important lessons, so We
can pick them, those that lure us with a meal and a warm bed, they lurk
scurrying back before it gets late
that is why We
bash and steal, seize opportunities at any cost when they arise, then strike
share the spoils, then indulge, spirits so high to not walk straight
our mantra, we spit off the edge of the world, echoing off derelict walls,
   'You, me, we!"
laugh, sing
indulge in sin,
sun rises, We
sleep. I see her thin
brown skin, she tells me she's a gin
from a big river town, now we
a team, my role from then on, protecting her from the jazz
of cruel customers, who now know her as Bella June
every year we
promise to get clean, with the cash she brings in, live like kings, not
   afraid to die
then one night the curlew cried, and I knew the phone would ring

soon

My list

Make words work, read Izumi Shikibu, breathe deeply
cherry blossoms and snow, tension
no two fires are the same but my intention to sit by it is
clock will continue to keep time without being watched
jade green bangle I have worn for years scrapes against the surface of the
laptop like chalk on a footpath
murmur of a teenager through the wall, fighting an imaginary battle
smell of slow cooked meat, tomatoes, and onion
warmth of the dog against my leg
with a whirl and pop of flame, a log falls against the side of the hearth
kindling splinters lay across the carpet
shoes left by the door
fan tucked away behind the chair from last summer
washing folded, not put away
Does anyone still grow chokos anymore?
I lifted the hem of my school uniform to carry them. My son doesn't
know what a choko is
car on the gravel driveway, neighbours home
their son will be off the school bus soon. His birthday is in July, I only
know this because balloons will be tied to the letter box in the coming
days. I wonder if he knows what a choko is?
faint bird call, and the dog shivers once more. The shadows dancing
across the carpet have grown long
cool air across my naked feet. I'm reminded that I own a cashmere scarf,
given to me by a past boyfriend. I still have it, but no word of him
dog sighs, son shouts they have won the war. He will be out of his room
soon looking for something to eat and complaining there is nothing in
the fully stocked cupboard and fridge
key in the front door

Two Pence

A tether of teeth
dead, torn, as titanium
 drill takes grip
turns room, tilted
red tender gums, toxic copper taste
slip, tattered and tired
holding tightly, gripping the dentists textured and tacky chair
threadbare carpet
time after time
he taps and taps
my throat gurgles, twitches
repairing the chipped tooth broken twice on tulip lip telephone mouthpiece
tiny snapdragons trumpeted mouths, tease from the polyester tie
continues to wipe tiny hands, trotters against his trousers
bruised thumb, traces around my tight lip, tackle hooked
taxing breath, tzatziki and tequila
nurse teases in twin set
talisman earrings, tease like tambourines
mood tigerish, inviting torrid amorous trysts
he turns a tomato hue
task completed
thighs push, thrust away the rusted trolley
payment tallied
and two pence tossed

Mango shortbread

Vapour trails line the sky
tracing journeys path
returning or leaving?

buckled in
oval windows and tea-stained carpet
check the pocket for a clue of
who last flew
used onboard flight stub
screwed up gum wrapper
Mango shortbread and bitter tea
no soy lite
I pretended to understand my role at the emergency exit

Behind the Scenes

Crack the spines of leather-bound registers
trace and retrace with fingertips
smooth down the pages
a trained eye finds the void
lingers
it's the space in between that demands attention

behind the scenes
objects lay unsure of purpose
until
swung
pressed
smoothed

fingers caress wounded shields
with bullet holes
armpit sweat is smeared across ochre on bark depicting mosquitos
whispered words leave saliva spit balls
on twisted fibres with
soft down feathers of the black swan from the Coorong

baaka canoe in dry dock
patiently waiting to dip once again into the sweet muddy waters
where the parntu glide past

tiddas' sing dirges
cradling gypsum with woven hair-net imprints
coated in white dust
released to go nowhere in the windowless room

a strand of hair found inside
caressed
an image of
blood dotting the nape of the neck
from worked stone scarring the scalp

on the cold slab in a dark concrete bunker
of the archaeology store
found, upturned
kicked along, broken by cattle or edging ornate garden beds
grinding stones once worked nardoo
women once laughed, winnowing in the sun

interactions in a safe blak space
like the wind running through the trees
falling, collecting the dust to twist and dance across claypans
one dies down, guides the smaller ones
encouraging them to twirl and dance with purpose

absent from the exhibition label
catalogue
archive
the record

Gathering

On the updraft of the mist
we gather
lineages, like a fine silk web that connect us
invisible to others, but taught to us as children
with the Welcome to this Country
I begin drawing the fine thread together
lyrebird and The Gully

we talk about ourselves
each of us percolating on names, places, Country
sifting through seaweed for precious rainbow kelp shells
in a room where I have sat before, I sit now sharing new conversations
we begin to crisscross, twist threads of commonalities and family ties
it is the start of our goolai
our small dilly bag which will hold this experience
inside we will place the learning and thoughts of this moment in time
to draw on later

    we look without talking, raise eyebrows, laugh and take shots at
      one another
    silence when we talk about histories that require no words
    silence needed to heal us at our most vulnerable
    days see us weave, pluck and pull at our threads
    stories plait, interlace

at midnight the moonlight glosses pines
on another night the wind picks up allowing past orators of Country
to fill our ears with language from the valley floor, feel Country on
bare skin

at the end of week our goolai will be complete and each one of us will
carry it with us on our journey
    filled with a chaplet of kookaburra and Black Cockatoo feathers,
    pages of knapped sentences, carved paragraphs, painted chapters
    and a bushel of native mint to keep us cleansed
we descend from the mountains to the plains
back across Countries
to new pathways, to continue weaving lineages, like a fine silk web
that connect us all

Afterword

Like Felicity Plunkett, I too believe that each of my poems has a secret addressee and in reading this collection, I hope you find your poem. I thank you for giving my words the chance to breathe.

Yellow Tailed Black cockatoos have just flown over and as always, I run to catch a glimpse. My dogs have learnt their cry and join me on the back deck. These birds often arrive marking key episodes in my life, including this last piece of writing for this collection. Makarra is reflected in my poems, rain nourishes my words, water cleanses my thoughts and refreshes the path of the life journey ahead of me.

The poems in this collection were written over the past few years in various locations: riverbanks; hospital corridors; writers retreats; oceans; in the leaf litter photographing fungi; by the fire with my two dogs; hotel rooms on business trips. I am inspired by all the poets that have walked beside me and have written words to fuel the fires for positive change and peace.

As I finish this afterword, the clouds have moved in and the makarra has arrived.

Notes

'Two Stroke': this poem is inspired by Jaya Savige's 'Hard Water'.

'Afternoon Light': this poem is inspired by Felicity Plunkett's 'Sea-Margins'.

'Kiira Kiira': *kiira-kiira*, *ngayi* and *wiimpatya* are Barkindji words for land, welcome and people.

'Cockatoos': *makarra* is a Barkindji word for rain.

'Baaka': *baaka* is a Barkindji word for the Darling River.

'Godoomba': *godoomba* is a Gundungurra/Darug word. I wrote this poem on their Country and took the spelling from the installation at Echo Point, Katoomba.

'Shifting': an ekphrastic poem commissioned by the National Gallery of Australia through Red Room Poetry.

'Windows': a poem influenced by Patricia Highsmith's, *The Cry of the Owl*.

'Grief is Love': *pinturas negras* refers to the works by Francisco Goya, one of my favourite collections and which I was fortunate to view at The Prado Museum in Madrid .

'Weerreewa': *weereewa* and *yuma* are Ngunnawal/Ngambri words. I wrote this poem on their Country on the foreshore of the lake.

'Suit of Lucency': an experiment in slicing and dicing the poems 'Mount Zion' by Ted Hughes and 'Moon Wrasse' by Willo Drummond.

'Picture Card': an experimental poem slicing and dicing the poems 'The Mob' by Omar Musa and 'Bushfire Love' by Jazz Money.

'Purple Stockings': a poem commissioned for the 2023 Assembly for the Future, *Unchartered Territory*.

'We': this poem is inspired by Gwendolyn Brooks' 'We Real Cool'.

'Mango Shortbread': this poem is influenced by Ellen van Neerven's found poem for her mum, and 'Mangoes'.

'Behind the Scenes': *tidda* is a word meaning sister and *parntu* is a Barkindji word for fish.

'Gathering': a reference to the Lyrebird and The Gully is influenced by the Welcome to Country at The Varuna Writers Centre in 2024. *Goolai* is a Ngemba word for woven bag. The Brewarrina Mission once stood on Ngemba Country.

Acknowledgments

I wish to thank my Mum, Jean South, who read to me as a child and for her guidance and unwavering love. My father, Barry South, who has guided my hand to pen my work, healing my heart from afar and in my dreams. I would like to thank my partner Roy Barker who throughout the many years has held me up to reach for the stars. My brother John South for discussing the arts, providing constructive feedback on the manuscript which kept me moving forward and for his stunning illustrations. My son Kaylan for whom I write and who has been my constant muse, especially for *The Gift*. Arthur and Minya who sat by my side on those cold Queanbeyan nights by the fire while I read, wrote and tested out my poetry, you deserve all those kisses and treats.

I would like to acknowledge that I write on Ngunnawal and Ngambri lands, thank Create NSW for providing financial support, and acknowledge the Gundungurra and Darug on whose lands the Varuna Writers Centre stands. It was at Varuna that the majority of the poems in this book were written. I would like to thank the Us Mob Writing group especially the late Kerry Reed-Gilbert, for the great nights out singing karaoke and telling me to keep writing. And the First Nations Aboriginal Writers Network where I have taken much inspiration from my sisters' and brothers' words.

I would like to thank Jeanine Leane, Felicity Plunkett and David Stavanger for being so generous with their time, and taking a genuine interest in my writing.

This debut collection would not have been possible without my publisher, Shane Strange, of Recent Work Press, and my editor, KA Nelson, who kept me afloat, provided editing advice, gently prodding but also giving me the space to enjoy the process.

And to all my friends who vowed with me to live our best lives and support each other in doing so—thank you.

It was through being selected to participate in the 2022 *Invisible Walls: poetry as a Doorway to Intercultural Understanding* program, run in partnership between the University of South Australia and Sogang

University in Seoul, South Korea, that I was encouraged to accelerate my writing practice, and hone my goals of being published and having my work widely recognised.

Over the past two years, several poems in this collection have been published, commissioned, read at workshops and writers' festivals, and discussed in interviews these include *Authora Australis*, *Kuracca Us Mob Writing First Nation Voices*, *The Rock Remain: Blak Poetry and story anthology*, *Duniyaadaari Journal*, Kolkata India, *Teesta Review: A Journal of Poetry*, Kolkata, India, *Rabbit: a journal for nonfiction poetry* and *Cordite Poetry Review*. I read at the *YES Campaign* for the Hon Anthony Albanese PM, *Lit Balm* Livestream Reading Series, New York USA, 2023 Blue Mountains Writers Festival *Red Room Poets Reading* plus *Us Mob Writing Reading*, 2023 *ACT Poetry Month Showcase Reading* at the National Gallery of Australia, 2024 National Folk Festival, 2024 Headlands Writers Festival. I was commissioned to write for the 2023 Assembly for the Future, *Unchartered Territory* and to write an ekphrastic poem for the National Gallery of Australia. 'Kurrajong' was commissioned by the *Kindred Trees* project (kindredtrees.com.au). I presented at the 2023 *Purrumpa First Nations Arts & Culture National Gathering*, Adelaide, South Australia and a conference paper at the 2024 International Symposium on Poetic Inquiry, Auckland New Zealand. In 2023, interviewed by Canberra ABC radio, ArtSound FM 92.7 *Poetry on the Radio* a two-part interview on my poetry practice and this year in *Cordite Poetry Review*.

My first piece of published writing for 2025 will be in *The Griffith Review*.

About the Author

Barrina South is a Barkindji woman living on Ngunnawal and Ngambri Country. As well as being an emerging poet, she is a visual artist and academic committed to Aboriginal women's autobiographical narratives. She has facilitated several workshops on her visual art and academic research arising from her MA (Hons) Sociology and BA Visual Arts.

Apart from being widely published, Barrina is an established Curator with a long career in both Federal and State cultural institutions, with experience in collection management, curatorial and public programs. More recently she has held senior roles in the New South Wales Public Service protecting and conserving Aboriginal and non-Aboriginal heritage, including the repatriation of ancestors back to Country.

Currently, Barrina is a member of the Canberra Critics Circle, establishing herself as a critic, as she believes there is an urgent need for more Aboriginal voices who can review and critique Indigenous written works, as well as those of non-Indigenous people. As a critic Barrina writes regularly for the *Canberra City News* and Arts Hub.

Barrina is passionate about politics and in her pursuit to effect positive change is standing as a candidate in the 2024 New South Wales Local Council elections for the Queanbeyan-Palerang local government area.

She acknowledges the many opportunities she has worked hard for, including those listed in the acknowledgements, but particularly values the experiences she enjoyed as Artist in Residence at the Sharjah Art Museum, Sharjah, United Arab Emirates and Swarovski Crystal World, Wattens, Austria.

www.ingramcontent.com/pod-product-compliance
Ingram Content Group Australia Pty Ltd
76 Discovery Rd, Dandenong South VIC 3175, AU
AUHW020639050325
407891AU00001B/1

9 781763 670105